Meditations

GRACE NOLL CROWELL

DEVOTIONS FOR WOMEN

ABINGDON PRESS

New York • *Nashville*

MEDITATIONS

Copyright MCMLI by Pierce & Smith

Library of Congress Catalog Card Number: 51-10747

H

SET UP, PRINTED, AND BOUND BY THE
PARTHENON PRESS, AT NASHVILLE,
TENNESSEE, UNITED STATES OF AMERICA

Foreword

It is a definite challenge to anyone to attempt to speak for and to the many capable Christian women of our land who lead the devotions in our churches or to write for those who are seeking inspiration for private worship.

Being keenly conscious of this challenge, I have undertaken the task humbly and prayerfully, longing to say the right word and only the right word.

I have not attempted it without going to a Higher Source for guidance. If the book proves helpful to anyone, I shall be grateful indeed.

GRACE NOLL CROWELL

Contents

1

The Glory Way

And an highway shall be there, and a way, and it shall be called The way of holiness; the unclean shall not pass over it; but it shall be for those: the wayfaring men, though fools, shall not err therein.
—Isa. 35:8

I said to one who stood at the world's far crossroads:
    "Which is the way that leads to eternal light?"
And he lifted his eyes to the hills ahead and answered:
    "Yonder it lies, and the Guide is still in sight."

"Who is this guide?" I asked, and he answered, "Jesus."
    "Who is this Jesus of whom I have never heard?"
And there to a worn, distressed, and bewildered comrade
    He told of the Saviour, word by precious word.

11

I left behind me the dark and troubled valley;
　　I took the road ahead, and I found him
　　　there:
A light to my feet, a radiance to my pathway,
　And ever within my heart I am aware

That I might have missed the way at the far-off
　　crossroads
　　If one had failed me who had the words to
　　　say,
And I shall cry aloud to each hesitant pilgrim:
　"Follow your Leader; follow the Glory Way."

WHAT a tragedy it would be for any fellow traveler to miss that beautiful straight way of holiness because one who knew the road had failed to direct him aright! There are countless ones today standing at the crossroads of the world, baffled and bewildered. Many in far lands have not so much as heard of the Christ. Many are confused by the many roads leading in different directions. To the unknowing the markers beside the way often seem inadequate, the posts broken, the lettering weathered and dim; and the pilgrims of earth come to some crucial point and either pleadingly ask the way or go stumbling blindly down the first road that seems most alluring.

What are we doing about it? Do we stand at attention, eager and ready to direct the inquiring one on the straight and narrow road ahead? Or do we who have been trusted with knowledge go on our way indifferent to the fate of our fellow man?

God grant that none we contact later on the way may say, "Why was I not told back at the crossroads of this Jesus? If one who knew the way had not failed me, I would not be in this Slough of Despond, this valley of despair. I too would be facing heavenward with the Guide ever in sight and the light shining silverly upon the road to the Eternal City."

We are told of a traveler in Norway who asked a small lad, "Son, which is the way to Oslo?"

The boy, pointing westward, replied, "Sir, I have never been to Oslo, but there is the road that leads to Oslo."

He did what he could. He did what you and I should be doing, pointing the way; and because of that certain directing the traveler may go forward, assured that ultimately he will arrive safely at his destination.

Jesus says, "I am the way, the truth, and the life." Let us point him out to every seeker, for he is the one true way. Let us say, "Yonder is your guide. Follow him. He is beckoning on. The path can never grow too steep when he leads on, and

no night can be so dark that his presence will fail
to light the way."

Our heavenly Father, the way of salvation lies
before us. Grant that we may ever be alert to direct
others aright. We praise thee that thou art our guide
at all times, and that whither thou goest, we can
safely go, assured that we will arrive at our destination at last. May we never be indifferent to the welfare of others. May our mission in life be the saving
of souls. We would not fail in that appointed work.
Help us, O Lord, that we may ever do thy will.
Amen.

2

Jewels

Then they that feared the Lord spake often one to another: and the Lord hearkened, and heard it, and a book of remembrance was written before him for them that feared the Lord, and that thought upon his name. And they shall be mine, saith the Lord of hosts, in that day when I make up my jewels; and I will spare them, as a man spareth his own son that serveth him.　　　—Mal. 3:16-17

WOMEN have ever been lovers of jewels—jewels that are the hidden treasures of God which men have ever delved to possess.

The crystal-clear sparkle of the diamond is dazzlingly beautiful. The ember-hearted ruby, the amethyst with its violet shadows, the sky-blue turquoise, the opal with its ever-changing fires, are so filled with light and color that no pen can paint them. It is natural indeed that women should love the unearthed and polished gems that are created by God's own hands.

15

Our scripture tells us that a true Christian may become a jewel in our Lord's magnificent collection; but in order to earn that award there is work to be done, even as miners must grapple for the precious stones deep in the old earth's mines.

The fear of the Lord is the first requisition. To love and serve him is another, and the third is this—we should think of him and speak often of his love and his saving power. We should "go tell [the] brethren." Only then will the great book be opened before him and our names written indelibly there, over which he may rejoice.

Do we fear the Lord as we should? Do we glorify his name upon every occasion? Are our thoughts ever largely concerned with the affairs of the kingdom? And this is most important— do we speak often with each other of our Lord?

What do women talk about as they meet? Is it not often of the weather, of world happenings, of neighborhood affairs, of our homes and our children, and much of the latest styles? How often do we greet each other with the Lord's name upon our lips? Do we call out as do the Alpine shepherds as they take their homeward way across the hills at evening, "Hitherto the Lord hath helped, let us praise him"? Do we say at Easter time as folk did of old, "The Lord is risen!" and does another make answer, "The Lord is risen, indeed"?

Perhaps these exact words would not be expected from us, but could we not "speak often one to another" of his goodness and mercy? Could we not come rejoicing over some answered prayer? Could we not give voice to his living promises when we see another distressed and discouraged? How often do we tell of the blessings which are direct from his hand? If we do so, we may be assured that the Lord "hearkens and hears it," that he is pleased, and that our names will be written in that great book which one day will be opened before him.

The time is brief. Why are we not more concerned with things eternal? We may well be amazed when we stop to consider how brief. We are here for a few short years and in eternity forever. If we knew we were going to move our family and household possessions to a far, strange country, would we not be thinking ahead of that land? Would we not tell our friends of our plans for the new life ahead? If we knew others would be joining us there, would we not be eager over that prospect?

The important thing is to tell others of the Eternal City. We are pilgrims and strangers in this land. May we speak often one to another of the kingdom of God in which we are to have a part.

Then in God's great heavenly mosaic we shall be accounted worthy to be his jewels, as beautifully clear and shining as are all precious gems. Oh, may we speak often of our Lord! May we fear him and love him and serve him as we go about our daily tasks, and may we think of him with grateful hearts and obedient minds. Thus we will be counted as true followers of the blessed Master.

To be a jewel in the Lord's collection
    Of brilliant gems that he has made his own
Will be a sacred privilege and honor
    As great as any heart has ever known.
And to have earned that rich and glorious title
    Because through life we often spake of him,
Will be reward beyond our brightest dreaming!
    God, grant we may be gems that will not dim
Before thy watchful eyes because we failed thee.
    Lord, we would often speak thy blessed name
And thus become thy everlasting jewels
    To burn before thee like clear living flame.

Our Lord, we do love thee; but too often we have failed thee. We come humbly asking thy forgiveness for our apparent indifference to thy glory. We would be mindful henceforth to speak often one to another of thy mercy and thy goodness, thy power and thy might. We would be bright jewels in thy heavenly kingdom, reflecting thy glory throughout eternity. Help us as women to be pleasing in thy sight. We ask this in thy Son Jesus' name. Amen.

3

For the New Year

In the beginning God . . . —Gen. 1:1

IN THE beginning God, and in the in-between, and throughout all eternity—forever there is God.

To be ever conscious of this truth is to make for fine, courageous Christian living. We feel God; we sense his living presence, and we would therefore do nothing to dishonor that great companion in our lives. We would love him and serve him as did the women of old who followed our Lord upon his earthly pilgrimage. Now, centuries later, we can be one with that goodly company of devout women, even in these strange and confusing times.

Let us be conscious at the beginning of this new year that nothing can separate us from God himself unless we do it of our own free will, and may he grant that we never do so.

Standing, as we do, between two eternities—the Past and the Future—our minds hark back as we recall Christ's words: "O Father, glorify thou me with thine own self with the glory which I had with thee before the world was."

God with Christ in the beginning of creation! God in Christ with us at the beginning of this new year! What a glory there is shining about us if we are eager and willing to do his will in the days to come!

That first beginning is all but too dazzling to contemplate—the suns and moons and stars splintering off in a blaze of glory, the world shaping beneath the hand of God—man emerging in God's own image.

Beginnings are incredibly important and beautiful. God gives them to us—a new day to begin again, a new year unsullied and clean.

We should study the chart that has been given us. Out of the glory God sent Christ to be our guide and compass. He has told us to come to him through that Son, who walked the earth and who knows so well the heart of humanity.

As we begin our work, let us go often to our heavenly Father, in the name of Jesus, as we ask for wisdom and guidance. He will not fail us. He has not failed us hitherto; he will not fail us now.

We must go to him when we grow discouraged

and disheartened at seemingly insurmountable
difficulties. We will find his promises glowing for
us like a home hearth fire by which we can warm
our hearts and our hands. It will light the way
and make plain our paths.

Great issues are at stake in the affairs of the
world. As women we can by studying our
Bibles learn how to pray effectively for the peace
for which we so much long. There will be problems arising in our community. We need to help
solve them. There will be important issues in
our church. Let us consult God often and meet
these issues according to his judgment. There
will be family crises to be met by each of us.
Only through prayer and faith and trust can they
be met successfully and wisely. For all these needs
to whom dare we go but to God?

Let us move forward valiantly, our hands in
his, and the way can never grow too dark or the
going be too rough if we have his strength and
his strong, unfailing light by which to travel.

The days lead out before our eyes,
　　The weeks and months where none have trod,
The unused year, a priceless gift
　　Directly from the hand of God.

O hearts, be glad; O hands, be clean;
　　O feet, be careful as you tread

The first clean, shining day that leads
  Into the year that lies ahead.

Thy priceless promised gift of days!
  How can we thank thee, God, unless
We bring within our hands some gift
  Of service that will cheer and bless

Those in great need—some singing faith,
  High courage, and the strength to lift
A comrade's load, and thus repay
  Thee, blessed Lord, for thy good gift.

Our gracious heavenly Father, hitherto thou hast
helped us on our way. Be with us still. May thy
presence illumine our days that there may be no
pitfalls for us, no paths to lead astray.

Bless thou our hurt, troubled world. Bless us as
a nation, that we may truly live up to our claim of
being a Christian nation. We would not shame thee
by our failure. Consider our immediate community.
May we have eyes to see the need near by and
answer that need with vital service. Be with us as
individuals, Lord, as we seek most earnestly to do
thy will. These things we ask in Jesus' name. Amen.

4

True Greatness

And it fell on a day, that Elisha passed to Shunem, where was a great woman; and she constrained him to eat bread. And so it was, that as oft as he passed by, he turned in thither to eat bread. And she said unto her husband, Behold now, I perceive that this is an holy man of God, which passeth by us continually. Let us make a little chamber, I pray thee, on the wall; and let us set for him there a bed, and a table, and a stool, and a candlestick: and it shall be, when he cometh to us, that he shall turn in thither. —II Kings 4:8-10

LET US pause awhile to consider one especially worthy woman of the Bible. Let us think of the Shunammite of long ago and the tribute paid to her in the Word of God.

We are told that "Elisha passed to Shunem, where was a great woman." Her dignity, her calm and quiet demeanor, and her steadfastness of purpose had established her splendid reputation far beyond her immediate vicinity. She was esteemed wherever her name was spoken.

Hers was a dignity inherent in all great souls who ever meet the crises of life with poise and courage. Who can think of the Shunammite without sensing her womanliness, her graciousness, her serenity, and above all her capability? She longed to serve the man of God who came as guest to her door, and she planned a way to do it. Like all good wives she consulted her husband first, and he evidently agreed, for the little room was erected upon the wall of their dwelling place —a small, clean room which contained simply the bare necessities, a bed, a stool, a table, and a candlestick. The Shunammite's hospitality was as simple and as natural as the fields beside her door, and her little house was as clean and unencumbered as the winds that ruffled the ripened wheat. One senses that she had ample time for study, for neighborliness, and for the doing of many kindly deeds.

She realized the prophet's need of relaxation after a hard day's travel over the countryside, teaching and preaching to the people that the "Lord he is God." She knew how essential it was for him to find rest and strength in solitude where he could commune with his Lord.

Where in all history can we find a woman more beautifully portrayed? It would be well if we would emulate her. Too often our own affairs grow burdensome with strange complexities. There are so many useless things within our homes and in our lives, and so many cares. Let us strive to simplify our living and thus leave more time for the work of God's kingdom here on earth. Let us recall that even in the Shunammite's later great perturbation she was enabled to meet this crisis with fortitude and high courage. When she was questioned, "Is it well with thee? is it well with thy husband? is it well with the child?" she answered simply, "It is well." And it was well, she knew, if the tragedy that had come upon her was according to God's will.

Oh, that we women today could make that same quiet answer as to the welfare of our households, both physically and spiritually! Oh, that we might ever live serenely with an unfaltering faith in the goodness of God and ever stand ready to serve him and our fellow man!

There are a great many women among us who deserve the same high tribute paid to the woman of Shunem long ago. The "great" are still with us—unselfish, tranquil, sincere, and loyal women who "go about doing good," who serve their church and their community and keep their homes fit places for the Invisible Guest. Let us honor them and praise them. God grant that more of us may live up to the high privilege of

Christian womanhood. Let us strive to go about our days serenely and gladly, rejoicing in the Lord and in the power of his might, and rejoicing that he has entrusted us with a great work to do.

Here is a tribute finer than any other;
   It was said of the Shunammite of long ago,
That wise and gentle woman, wife and mother,
   To whom the Prophet turned when he must go
      into a strange and far-off land where he
Had need of gracious hospitality.

Today as we review the splendid living
   Women of the earth, the mothers, wives,
Who pray and spend their days in selfless giving,
   In ever-ready sharing of their lives
Through this the world's dark hour of desperate
     need,
These too are women who are great indeed.
Let us pause awhile considering the worth
Of the blessed Christian womanhood of earth.

Dear Lord, we come to thee most earnestly beseeching thee to give us a clearer vision of life as it should be lived. Help us to simplify our complex lives, to be more serene and tranquil, more filled with quiet joy, that we may be better fitted to serve thee aright. We too long to be great in thy sight. Help us to the accomplishment of this end, we pray in Jesus' name. Amen.

5

The Races of the Earth

Thus speaketh the Lord of hosts, saying, Execute true judgment, and shew mercy and compassions every man to his brother. —Zech. 7:9

Who is there dare say that one race stands
Superior to another, that God's hands
Move favorably for one and not another?
Who can say, "This one man is my brother
And not that one"? The black men think of
    Christ
As black of skin. To them he has sufficed
As Saviour, and the yellow race may claim
A yellow Jesus with a Chinese name,
While he, the Father of us all, looks down
Upon each land, the country and the town,
And sees his children, and he loves us all.
Who am I to stand aloof and call
My brother or my sister less than I?
We are one family here beneath God's sky,
With one Father and one heavenly home above.
Lord, help us reach all races with our love.

TODAY from stark necessity we have been shocked into taking cognizance of the far reaches of the earth and the many races thereon. Too long we have been complacent in our attitude toward the world and its peoples. Hitherto it has been a nebulous thing. Far-off China meant nothing much to us—that great overpopulated land with its millions of underfed and underprivileged, its high and low castes, its squalor and its splendor. Africa? So far away that we could scarcely visualize its vast interior with its dark inhabitants slinking through dense jungles, the throbbing beat of tom-toms, the miasmic mists and burning fevers, a land and a people so remote we left them largely to God and to themselves and to the few great-souled missionaries who have gone to spend their lives for the "least of these."

To be sure we have helped support these laborers with our tithes and offerings, which have often been inadequate. We have prayed for the missionaries and those they are striving to save, but not earnestly enough and not often enough. But strangely today the world has drawn as close to us as our breathing. What concerns the black and the yellow races of the earth concerns us, and most vitally. It has become a terrifying, doom-threatening reality, this world of wars and rumors of wars with the complexity of its governments.

Many nations are toppling, and so closely are

we linked with them that we also shall fall if we do not turn in great throngs to God, imploring him for mercy in this immediate and alarming crisis. Too long we have forgotten our brothers and our sisters. We have been complacent in thinking that ours is a Christian nation especially blest of God. What a pity! The first qualifications of a true Christian should be the love of God and a passionate love for his fellow men.

Long ago in Galilee, Jesus told us what to do. He said, "Go ye therefore, and teach all nations, baptizing them in the name of the Father, and of the Son, and of the Holy Ghost: . . . and, lo, I am with you alway even unto the end of the world."

Have we been as zealous as he desires us to be? Have we done all we could? He knows the answer by looking into our hearts—and so do we.

He spent his earthly years teaching us to love our fellow men. Had we loved *enough*, the world would have been a vastly different place in which to live. There are men and women giving their very life's blood to carry out the command of the Master. They are laboring diligently in foreign fields seeking to find and save the lost. But as laymen have we done our utmost to help? If we could not go, have we sent? Alas! We have not even solved the racial problems in our own immediate communities!

Let us begin to pray as never before for wisdom and guidance that we may so lift Christ up that he can draw all men to him. Then there will be no North, no South, no East, no West, but a united kingdom upon the earth with one King and Ruler of us all.

James says: "If any of you lack wisdom, let him ask of God, that giveth to all men liberally, and upbraideth not; and it shall be given him." Let us be much in prayer for our troubled world today. Let us pray that through the wisdom God has promised to give all seeking ones we may be enabled to help him to set up his kingdom upon the earth, where all peoples may come to worship the only true and living God.

Gracious Lord, we grieve to acknowledge our many failures. We have been remiss in so often failing to do the things that thou wouldst have us do. We thank thee that as we come asking for wisdom, so may we better deal with all peoples wisely and well; that thou dost not upbraid us for our shortcomings, but that thou art pleased and willing to work with us for the good of all mankind.

Help us to realize that all men are our brothers and all women are our sisters, and that thou art the Father of us all. May we become a great united family that will find the peace for which we so long have sought as we kneel together to love and serve and honor thee. We ask in Jesus' name. Amen.

6

The Alabaster Box

Now when Jesus was in Bethany, in the house of Simon the leper, there came unto him a woman having an alabaster box of very precious ointment, and poured it on his head, as he sat at meat. But when his disciples saw it, they had indignation, saying, To what purpose is this waste? For this ointment might have been sold for much, and given to the poor. When Jesus understood it, he said unto them, Why trouble ye the woman? for she hath wrought a good work upon me. . . . Verily I say unto you, Wheresoever this gospel shall be preached in the whole world, there shall also this, that this woman hath done, be told for a memorial of her.
—Matt. 26:6-10, 13

She hath done what she could.—Mark 14:8

TODAY if our love for Christ is great enough, and if we are on fire for the salvation of souls, we too have a precious alabaster box in our hands ready to break for our Lord's sake.

The spikenard it contains is very precious and costly, for it is the attar of a good woman's heart —her devotion, her selflessness, her untiring service. It is the crushing of a thousand petals that represent many hours of earnest endeavor in the fields of our Lord.

We gather these petals, and we bring them to him humbly. We break the box, and the fragrance rises, a rich savor before him; and we may be certain that he will accept it.

How wonderful it must have been that far-off day when the woman, breaking her cherished box, heard him say, "She hath done what she could"! He will say that of us if we too do all we can do for him. Let us praise his name for his mindfulness ever of us and of our accomplishments.

To deserve his commendation we must earn it. It means not lip service alone. It means carrying the light to those in darkness. It means true missionary zeal. It means self-sacrifice in the giving of ourselves and of our means to others that they may come to know the one true and living God. It means earnest prayer and heartfelt praise. It means working together as a unit for the salvation of the world.

The contents of the alabaster box are truly priceless. Have we one in our hands today? Are we willing to go out and gather the flowers from among the thorns and thistles of the fields that they may be crushed as a special offering to our Lord? Are we ready to be crushed ourselves that others may be resurrected?

Let us endeavor to be more diligent, more earnest, through these days when the world is troubled and perplexed The time is brief. A lifetime is such a little while, and there is so much to be done. Let us be quick in the giving of ourselves. Let us be swift in reaching out to those whose hearts are yearning for the living Christ. Let us ever keep tryst with God himself.

Christ said: "Whosoever this gospel shall be preached in the whole world, there shall also this, that this woman hath done, be told for a memorial of her." Would it not be a blessed reward to have this unseen box which we bear in our hands today become a memorial for us and our time and on through eternity? Would it not be worth every effort we make to gather the incense of right living, the fragrance of good deeds together in this rare box and break it before him as a love offering to him, our Saviour? Would it not be worth a lifetime of earnest endeavor to have him say of us, "She hath done what she could"?

The women of the Bible ever served
  As earnestly as we would serve today.

Dorcas was "full of good works," we are told,
  And "almsdeeds which she did" along her way.
Lydia, seller of purple, filled her hours
  With useful beauty; Anna served with prayer
And fasting as she moved with quiet grace
  Among the dim aisles of the temple there.

While Martha had a privilege so great
  And beautiful we all might envy her;
To serve the Master in one's own small home
  Should truly set the strongest heart astir.
So would we serve today in church and home,
  And so we too would toil with dignity,
Conscious of the great importance, Lord,
  Of a woman's work when it is done for thee.

Our heavenly Father, we would bring our alabaster boxes to thee. They are filled with the fragrance of good deeds and kindly words. We would kneel at thy feet and crave forgiveness when we have done amiss. We pray thee for thy guidance and thy wisdom as we seek to do thy will. Accept our offerings as we break them before thee, and grant, our Father, that we too may receive thy commendation as did Mary of old. We pray always in thy precious Son's dear name. Amen.

7

Now Is the Time

For he saith, I have heard thee in a time accepted,
and in the day of salvation have I succoured thee:
. . . behold, now is the day of salvation.
—II Cor. 6:2

Say not ye, There are yet four months, and then
cometh harvest? . . . Lift up your eyes, and look on
the fields; for they are white already to harvest.
—John 4:35

A RETURNED explorer made a strange and startling
statement that burns its way like flame through
the consciousness of the reader, coming as it does
after centuries of striving by the Church to
bring the knowledge of Christ to the entire
world. The explorer said: "Within twenty-five
years man has arrived at the uttermost ends of
the earth. The world of today contains not a
single hidden city, dark continent, nor impenetrable desert. Thus the romance of the ages
draws to an end."

Now that the door is wide open, there is no impenetrable wilderness on the face of the earth where the word of God cannot be carried. The time is at hand for the full salvation of mankind. God will not have it otherwise. He will work for it, and he will work with us to bring it to pass.

This is a critical hour in the world's history, and we as Christians must meet the demands made upon us. We should shoulder our share of the responsibility and move triumphantly forward in Christ's name to accomplish the greatest task ever set for mankind. The church people are being awakened as never before. God grant that we may be found worthy of such a trust!

It is coming! Hark, the sound is on the air!
    It rolls like thunderous waves across a sea—
The tramp of millions drawn from everywhere
    In the great advance of Christianity.
They come, these followers of the living Christ,
    Marching with their lifted flags unfurled;
They bring a gift that never could be priced
    To a hurt, bewildered, and chaotic world—
A world whose chaos man himself has wrought,
    A world that flounders in its dark despair.
They offer that which lands have ever sought
    And failed to find unless the Christ be there.
And now they come, these great onrushing
      throngs,

Aflame with God, with a will that does not
cease,
To bring salvation and to right the wrongs
Of all the world in desperate need of peace.

A great many churches have been destroyed
through war. It is vastly important that each
one of them should be rebuilt upon its eternal
foundation. Christ said, "Upon this rock I will
build my church; and the gates of hell shall not
prevail against it."

If today anyone is tempted to stand beside
those blasted walls and wail, "The church is
dead!" let him remember the Master's emphatic
words concerning his Church. Its granite lies
deeper than the earth itself. It is impervious to
shock. It is unshakable now, and throughout
eternity nothing can corrode it or tear it apart.
It is our place to rebuild the outer edifices that
Christ's work can be carried triumphantly forward.

Denominations everywhere realize the full importance of sending missionaries to the far
corners of the earth. Thousands are being sent,
but thousands more are needed. It is said that
every boat departing from our shores carries workers for the kingdom and that many airplanes are
bearing great concourses of trained men and
women who are willing and ready to be spent

in the cause of Christ. The call has come from Japan alone for a thousand missionaries to save its needy people; and it must be answered, for this is God's own voice calling.

We find in his Word this statement: "Ye are a chosen generation, a royal priesthood, an holy nation, a peculiar people; that ye should shew forth the praises of him who hath called you out of darkness into his marvellous light." Should we not so live that these words could truly be spoken of us? Should we not be a "peculiar people," ready and eager to show others the beauty of holiness and to make every attempt to lead them "into his marvelous light"?

World missions are in the heart of the people as never before. We must be ready instruments in the redemption of mankind. This means you, and it means me; for truly we must be laborers together with God to accomplish this great undertaking.

"How then shall they call on him in whom they have not believed? And how shall they believe in him of whom they have not heard? and how shall they hear without a preacher?" How shall they indeed? The question echoes in our ears like a reiterating voice. How shall they hear unless we go or send? What a responsibility and what a privilege for the Christian women of our land! With the way now opened we can see that they do hear.

The persecution of churches abroad has brought about a world-wide wave of denunciation. Religious freedom is so vital and precious that men will fight for it to the death if need be. It will be a victorious fight, for God wills it to be so. He will not be mocked.

Let us get right in our individual lives. Let us strengthen our churches at home and abroad by the renewal of spiritual zeal and by the education of our youth for Christian service. Let us raise the necessary funds for mission work, and may we undergird our giving with earnest prayer and with the gospel of Jesus Christ. Then shall we truly be followers of our heavenly Father here upon earth.

Lord God, we are marching ahead with thee, and there can be no falling behind, no breaking of ranks, and no failure with thee as our guide in this great undertaking of the salvation of souls. Bless, we pray thee, the efforts being made to further thy kingdom on earth. So bless us that all we plan and hope to do may be accomplished. This we ask in thy Son Jesus' name. Amen.

8

Compassion

Finally, be ye all of one mind, having compassion one of another, love as brethren, be pitiful, be courteous. —I Pet. 3:8

OCCASIONALLY we come upon an unusually arresting verse in our Bible study. We may have read that verse often, but with holden eyes and a closed mind. However, when the full meaning of the words penetrates our consciousness, they stand out like a collection of rare jewels under lamplight.

Such is our scripture today, and the jewels shine before our eyes crystal-clear and beautiful. Peter admonishes us, "Be ye all of one mind." What dissension would be avoided if we always were agreed on the real issues of life! How blessed would be our meetings together and with what harmony through the hours!

Christ says, "Where two or three are gathered together in my name, there am I in the midst

41

of them." To have him in our midst is to have
unlimited power to draw upon. To have us all of
one mind, and that mind turned toward him for
wisdom and guidance, would work miracles.
There would be no limit to what any group
gathered together in his name could do.

Then Peter goes on to say, "Having compassion one of another." Compassion is the kernel
of right living. The word itself is one of the
most beautiful in any language. It means tenderness and sympathy for others in any distress or
misfortune. It means sharing one another's
burdens and thus fulfilling the law of Christ. It
means helping others in their suffering or sorrow
to the very best of our ability. In a compassionate
heart there can be no ill will, no malice toward
any comrade on the road. Oh, may we ever be
moved with compassion at the sight of another's
need! May we take on something of the white
flame of pity that burned in the heart of Christ
as he walked upon the earth and beheld humanity
bowed beneath heavy loads.

We are told to "love as brethren." Where
love abides, there can be no hatred, no coveting;
for we are told on good authority that "love
suffereth long, and is kind; love envieth not; love
vaunteth not itself, is not puffed up, doth not
behave itself unseemly, seeketh not its own, is not
provoked, taketh not account of evil." And we

are told to love one another even as our heavenly Father loves us.

There would be blessed harmony on the earth if we all loved as we should. What freedom from ill would there be if we only loved enough. There would be no self-seeking, no evil spoken; for there would be no evil in the mind and heart. How clear and clean would be the atmosphere in any group if love reigned there! And there would be no poison-fanged gossip with its death dealing to hurt anyone. There would be no misunderstandings and slights which all too often occur when women meet together. God help us to love each other as we should! God help us to heed his wise admonitions!

And Peter continues, "Be pitiful." These two brief words express much. "Have pity," they say, "for all misfortune and all unfortunates, and with that pity reach out helpful and healing hands to succor those in distress." Pity, like faith, without works is dead and worse than dead. Let us be tenderhearted in our pity, so much so that we will be impelled to act for the betterment of our kind. Let us have eyes to see and ears to hear the cry of need everywhere. Let us have hearts that will not rest until we do our best to aid the hurt and bewildered ones about us. We recall that Christ said, "Inasmuch as ye have done it unto one of the least of these my brethren, ye have done it unto me."

Our lives should be given over to the purpose of serving the Lord through our fellow men; this is his desire. It should be our full-time aim through these especially trying days upon the earth.

And now we are told, "Be courteous." Dictionaries define the word "courteous" as "of courtly politeness," but at the heart of it there is a warmer and lovelier meaning. The root of kindness is tenderness, benignity, and good will toward others. It has been said that the thoughtful person has no real need of a book of etiquette. One who is inherently kind is ever polite, and his manners need no schooling.

To be courteous is to be kind, and to be kind is to be courteous. To be polite means simply to be kind to others and thoughtful for their comfort, to place their well-being ahead of one's own. Courtesy means good breeding. It makes a gentleman of a commoner and a true lady of the plainest and most unassuming woman.

Let us be courteous in all our dealings with others. Let us endeavor to make the best of ourselves that the world in which we live may be a better place. Let us be loving, pitiful, and above all let us be compassionate. Let us have sympathy one for another, and may we use the best judgment possible as we strive to express that sympathy lest some jarring word we say may hurt another already hurt overmuch.

Sympathy is your hurt within my heart;
   O Friend, may I come in and take your hand
And say a healing word and have a part
   In this your grief? How well I understand!
For I have gone the whole long weary way;
   I know how steep the slopes, how rough the
      road;
But also, Friend, I know there comes a day
   When God's own hand will lift your heavy
      load.
Take heart!—Tomorrow's hills will shine with
      light,
   And happiness again will lave your breast.
Have faith and know that after this dark night
   Will come release and peace and needed rest.
Trust now, and God, whose Word is ever true,
Is sure to reach a hand to comfort you.

Our dear Lord, we realize that life needs much the soothing oil of sympathy and compassion. It needs the healing power of love and the graciousness of true courtesy. May we study to show ourselves approved unto thee at all times. Dwell thou within us. Be the guest of our hearts, and may we never offend thee by our words or our ways. With thou as our mentor, Lord, may we ever grow more like thee. Amen.

9

The Presence

And he said, My presence shall go with thee, and I will give thee rest. —Exod. 33:14

Surely the righteous shall give thanks unto thy name: the upright shall dwell in thy presence. —Ps. 140:13

Call unto me, and I will answer thee, and shew thee great and mighty things, which thou knowest not. —Jer. 33:3

THE HUMAN heart is essentially lonely. Happiness cannot be completely shared; sorrow must be borne within the confines of the breast, and truly all suffering is lonely. One's body is a universe within itself, holding a spirit that runs every gamut of human emotion, which can never be fully expressed nor comprehended by even our nearest and dearest.

But—and this is our salvation and our stay— there is a presence that never leaves or forsakes us.

Forever there is the Holy Spirit dwelling within all who will accept and receive him. He is that "other Comforter whom Jesus prayed the Father to give us—one who will abide with us through storm and stress as well as through days of joy and thanksgiving. The loving Christ could not and would not leave his children comfortless.

"My presence shall go with thee," he says, and that companionship is and will be sufficient lifelong to all who will claim it.

There is a famous painting by a great artist that touches and yet strengthens the heart. The setting is a vast cathedral drawn deep in shadows. A fire burns flickeringly upon the altar. The great pillars catch a glow from the lighted candles. The pews are dark and empty, seemingly growing darker at the entrance of the cathedral. There a lone woman kneels outside the last pew. Evidently she felt herself unworthy to have gone farther into the room or into the pew. She is merely a dim figure shrouded in darkness, and her attitude of agonizing supplication is so marked it pulls at the heartstrings.

The beauty of the painting lies in the "Presence." The Christ stands back of the woman, unseen by her yet making his presence felt. His head is circled with pale light; his entire body seems to be pulsing from some inner glow. And suddenly we are comforted, knowing that the

answer to the woman's pleading is near at hand—
so close that she can reach out and lay hold of it.
We recall his words, "Call unto me, and I will
answer thee, and shew thee great and mighty
things, which thou knowest not."

How many women throughout the ages have
wept in churches and in the pews of cathedrals,
praying in agony for some great need of their
hearts! How many have felt nearer to the Christ
there than anywhere else on earth! The church
is the Father's house, and there we can feel close
to him. We sense his presence reaching out to us
with wounded hands to comfort and sustain us.
His voice can be heard more clearly there if one
but listens. Hark! It is sounding softly through
the temple of our souls: "I will . . . shew thee
great and mighty things, which thou knowest
not."

Oh, the countless ones who have been shown
those things through answered prayer! Oh, the
heartaches and the heart longings that have been
lessened and healed and the joy restored by the
unseen yet never failing Presence waiting there
in the shadows to comfort and bless all who cry
to him!

Today we need to remember the quiet power
that is working in and for us. It is good to kneel
and tell him the desires of our hearts and the
great needs of our souls. We may be assured of

his wise understanding. We may be sure he will help us. Above all we may be certain of his nearness at all times. Praise his holy name!

Let us never forget that we are anchored in his power. We can lean on his arms that never tire. He will permeate our weakness with his strength. His love will sustain us. We can open our hearts that may have been shrinking with fear, and he will instill bravery and courage there. Our loneliness will be lifted by a living, breathing presence. There will ever be the Comforter, who was sent down from heaven to abide within each and every one who believes on the name of the Lord and Saviour Jesus Christ.

Lord, I believe, I kneel, I pray, I plead,
    And all the while within the shadowed gloom
I know there is a strength to meet my need
    Within the close seclusion of this room.
I have these hands to touch thy garment's hem;
    There is thy virtue flowing out to me
And thy compassion that does not condemn
    My often weak and faltering trust in thee.

Thy presence, Lord, is with me; I can feel
    Thy love like some lamp lit within my breast.
I shall be quiet, Lord, now as I kneel
    And wait thy will. Then rising, truly blest,
My heart shall praise thee throughout all the way
That thou does lead me day by passing day.

Gracious heavenly Father, in the temple of our souls we crave the blessing of thy presence. We would do no unworthy thing to make thee ashamed to draw near us as we pray. Come as our guest and comforter that we may ever sense thy nearness, even if our human sight be too holden to see thee standing in the shadows keeping watch over us.

Grant us thy matchless power that we may be able to make others aware of thee as they wait upon thee in prayer. This we ask in our Lord Jesus' name. Amen.

10

One Day at a Time

Therefore I say unto you, Take no thought for your life, what ye shall eat, or what ye shall drink; not yet for your body, what ye shall put on. Is not the life more than meat, and the body than raiment? Behold the fowls of the air: for they sow not, neither do they reap, nor gather into barns; yet your heavenly Father feedeth them. Are ye not much better than they? —Matt. 6:25-26

Take therefore no thought for the morrow: for the morrow shall take thought for the things of itself. Sufficient unto the day is the evil thereof. —Matt. 6:34

As thy days, so shall thy strength be.—Deut. 33:25

LET US as women today discuss our shortcomings. If there is one who does not need the admonition of our Lord, she should stand as a shining light and let us witness an example of faith and beautiful trust.

In these days when the world seems to be one great sea of unrest, when we are harassed by unprecedented demands, when we grow weary and worn with the struggle of living, the Lord has given us a sure cure for care in these verses of scripture.

Of course he does not mean us to be improvident with our means nor slatternly in our appearance, but what he really is saying is this: Build an invisible fence around today, and stay within that enclosure. Do not try to look beyond it, and live your life the best you can moment by moment, prayerfully, earnestly, joyfully, and I will be with you. He assures us of strength for one day and for only one day. He will supply tomorrow's strength when that day comes. "As thy days, so shall thy strength be." This is his magnificent promise. Let us believe him and trust him within the confines set between dawn and night, and let us serve him through the hours to the very best of our ability.

We do not need to be told how much vital energy is wasted through anxious thought and by looking ahead with apprehension. How greatly we are weakened through bearing burdens we have no need of shouldering through the heat of the day. When we forget the Lord's admonitions, it is simply a matter of lack of trust and faltering faith. How it must grieve him!

How can we live more victoriously? How can we make our day pleasing to him? Only through prayer, for no one is strong enough to face a day alone. We may have to break a lifetime habit of anxiety over the future. We may have to break the day into small bits. We may have to take ourselves severely in hand and recall to mind each precious promise of God concerning the way he wants us to live. We may fail at times; but if we are persistent, with God's help we shall conquer the bugaboo of fear and apprehension which we have no right to entertain within our day's enclosure.

We want most earnestly to be worthy servants of our Lord. We long to be good citizens, to be a bulwark to our church and in our homes. We can be these things only if we are geared to our best. Life is made up of days, and we are their inhabitants. Let us walk through them courageously and helpfully in the strength of the Lord, and thus we will become a force hitherto undreamed of in our world today. God help us to live worthily.

The day leads out before us hour by hour;
   Lord, we would live it beautifully with thee,
For only through thy strength and by thy power
   Can we move forward bravely, fearlessly.

We would not conjure lions in the way,
  Nor fear the tasks that wait for us to do;
Only one day, dear Lord, one little day,
  Is not too long for us to travel through.

Tomorrow has no claim upon us, Lord;
  We have no promise for tomorrow's strength.
All that we ask, according to thy Word,
  Is strength and wisdom for today's brief length.

Lord God, help us to attain the high pinnacle of peace of mind and strength of body and soul which thy Word promises. Too often we have been guilty of the things that thou hast cautioned us against—anxiety, fear, and the bearing of needless burdens.

Help us to clear out the thorns and brambles that have often detained us on our forward march. They have cluttered our pathway. They have torn and hurt us. May we destroy them and plant instead the seeds of tranquillity, the seeds of kindness, of faith, and of buoyant hope. Thus may we be strong and pleasing servants in thy garden of life. We ask thy help always in the name of Jesus. Amen.

Peace of Mind

——————————————————

Thou wilt keep him in perfect peace, whose mind is stayed on thee: because he trusteth in thee. Trust ye in the Lord for ever: for in the Lord Jehovah is everlasting strength.   —Isa. 26:3-4

WERE ANY serious-minded Christian today asked the question, "What quality should you chose first to possess in your spiritual life?" I believe the thoughtful one would answer, "Peace of mind."

Even before peace of body, which means comforting freedom from pain, peace of mind should be pre-eminent. We are told how to obtain that peace in such simple and direct language that even a child can understand and heed it.

We are to stay our minds on God because we trust him. Could anything be clearer? How simple it is, and how marvelously he does his part when we do ours!

When we trust him fully and completely,

day by day, year in and year out, we are staying our minds on the most powerful force in all the universe, the unfailing power of God. Trust means assured reliance on another's integrity and justice. Trust is confidence in his willingness and ability to perform that which he promises.

Nothing can move the one who trusts his God with all his heart. Nothing can make him afraid, for he is linked to one all-powerful. The word "trust" is as beautiful as the word "peace," but in a different way. Trusting is our part; peace is the gift of God.

In all the world of letters there is no more meaningful and significant word than "peace." By what devious ways does mankind seek to obtain it, and how often we fail because we do not trust in the one power that can produce it! I trust that this poem may make the finding of true peace simpler for some bewildered one:

> I prayed for peace, and God delayed
> The answer to the prayer I prayed.
> I thought it something he would share
> From his great store, and so my prayer
> Went daily up that I might know
> The singing joy, the warmth, the glow
> Of peace that someway I had lost.
> But now I know we pay the cost
> For everything that we hold dear.
> I read God's Word, and it is clear

That peace comes only when the heart
Is stayed on him. The staying part
Must be my own, and I must cease
My doubts and fears, then perfect peace
Is promised. Dear God, help me stay
My wayward heart on thee today.

Truly he has promised peace to the troubled heart and mind, and we know "there hath not failed one word of all his good promise." Let us keep remembering this vital truth. The serene Christian is the helpful one. She accomplishes more in the Lord's service than does the distracted and anxious one. She moves with confidence and assurance, for she is ever conscious of that promised inner strength. His wisdom and his power she knows are hers, ever working through and for her.

The one who has lost her anchor drifts hither and yon, played upon by every vagrant wind that blows. She accomplishes nothing, for she is not moving forward toward the goal that our heavenly Father has set for us in our Christian living.

Our church societies, our neighborhoods, our homes, have great need of the women who have stayed their minds on God—have so stayed them that nothing can move them from their direct and forward course in the service of the peerless Christ. Let us study to be quiet. Let us ever listen for the voice that will surely direct us if we are attuned to his Word, and may the peace of God which passeth all understanding be with us one and all forevermore.

Lord God, thou hast promised that if any lack wisdom, let him come to thee. We come, Father, today. Many times we have failed to trust thee as we should; often our minds have been tempest-tossed when they should have been filled with thy peace. Move among us, Lord, as thus didst long ago on a night of storm, and speak peace. Then and then only shall we come into our desired haven. We thank thee, Lord, and we praise thy holy name for all thy tender mercies to us thy children. Amen.

12

Rest

Come away by yourselves to a lonely place and
rest a while.   —Mark 6:31 (R.S.V.)

THERE is much stress laid upon women's activities
in the church and in the home and in professional
life. So much is said of them that one is inclined
to think that work is the all-important issue of
life. It is important, and vastly so, but Jesus, the
sanest person who ever walked the earth, the most
poised and physically perfect, spoke often of the
need of rest.

If he required it, and he did, how much more
so is our need for the replenishment of our life
forces through these complex days!

We recall that he was ever conscious of the
frailties of humanity. He was ever considerate of
all whom he met. When the throngs pressed hard
about him, when they spent long hours with him
after they had followed him for miles out of town,
he bade them sit down upon the cool green grass

and rest while he performed the miracle of the loaves and fishes for their welfare.

He found it decidedly necessary to slip away to the mountainside apart, there to be with God. He would spend hours in quiet communication with the Father, and then he would return to his arduous duties, refreshed and renewed in mind and body.

Our work often suffers from the lack of efficiency caused by fatigue. There is a great work to be done. God expects us to do it, but to him it is all-important that his children have sufficient rest in order to carry on that work.

We need to follow his admonition and his example at all times. When we do so, we are safe. We too need often to go apart and be with God, seeking his wisdom and his guidance, in order that we may be better equipped for his service.

A great man of our nation was speaking of his early boyhood. He told of the influence of his Christian mother upon his entire life. He said that her days were unusually busy ones, full to overflowing with the cares of her household and with her many outside activities. She was a farmer's wife, the mother of a large family with never-ending demands upon her time and her strength. She was a good neighbor and a capable church worker in a church where there were few workers.

He recalled her leaving her household tasks undone as she went immediately after breakfast to her small upstairs room. He said her children all knew their mother had gone there to read her Bible and to pray, and that under no circumstances was she to be disturbed.

"I never saw her irritated," he said. "I never saw her disturbed by the clamoring demands awaiting her upon her return from that quiet and profitable hour. She took up her day's burdens with serenity, and she walked through the hours with a steadfast strength and faith. She seemed to be sustained by some inner certainty as to life itself, which came, we knew, from that quiet while alone with God and his Word."

We can rest assured that her children were well cared for, that her little house was kept clean and shining, and that her church and her neighbors never called upon her for help in vain. What a blessed memory to give to a child! What a heritage to leave behind!

"Come away by yourselves . . . and rest a while." The call is as clear today as it was when Christ first uttered it centuries ago. Let us heed its admonition. We will be abler workers, better women in our communities, better wives and mothers, and better in any profession we may enter. "Learn of me," the Master said. Oh, may we con well the lessons that he has given us!

He went about doing good. He taught the great multitudes. He healed the sick. Virtue went out of him to others. In order that his spent strength might be renewed he rested. His philosophy was as simple as that.

We women often spend our strength until the fires of our spirit burn out and need to be replenished. We work to the point of exhaustion and fall in a leaden sleep at night, rising again almost as tired as we were the day before. We awaken to the bewilderment of another demanding day, often without the sustaining power of God's Word and without taking time to hear his voice speaking clearly as we will hear it if we wait upon him.

Let us take time for rest. Let us go apart with God in order to move among our kind more helpfully, happily, serenely, and thus accomplish mighty things for and with our Lord.

Out of the peace and quiet of an hour
   Alone with God, may come a wealth so great
That any heart can find a hidden power
   Undreamed of hitherto: the power to wait
His blessed will or power to rise and go
   Into a hard-pressed battle for the right,
Or it can give the impetus to grow
   Out of the hindering darkness into the light.

As Christ himself felt deep and vital need
   Of many a quiet waiting while alone
With God the Father who had food to feed
   All hunger that men's souls had ever known,
So would I seek him in some place apart,
   Some quiet spot where I can hear him speak
His words of wisdom to my waiting heart,
   And there find strength and comfort that I
     seek.

Lord God, we need thy companionship above that of all others. Meet us daily in some still place where we may be alone with thee. Teach us how best to order our lives. Speak often with us, we pray, that we may come to know thee better. Help us to grow in knowledge and wisdom that we may serve thee aright. We ask this in Jesus' name. Amen.

13

Obstacles

I will make all my mountains a way.—Isa. 49:11

WAS THERE ever any earnest, sincere woman who did not find apparent mountains in the way of some righteous endeavor? Often they may be from lack of physical strength upon her part, or her family may oppose any outside activities such as community service or work in the church, work that she is longing wistfully to accomplish. Or perhaps there may be some obstacle placed in her way by God because he sees she is better fitted to travel another road.

But God has said, "I will make *all* my mountains a way." He has promised to be with us all the appointed days. How marvelous is this promise! It proves definitely his loving watchfulness over us as we travel life's highroads. It is blessed to know that the days are appointed unto us to do his will in the land of the living. It is not a haphazard plan but a thoughtfully appointed one, and we may rest assured that the God who cares enough for us to plan our days for us is interested in how we live those days.

If he erects an impassable barrier in our forward going, we can be certain that he will open up another and better way for us on our heavenward climb, and the mountains ahead which look so difficult to surmount will become a way to the glorious things we long to accomplish for our Lord. He has promised, and he will "make a way" for us.

Obstacles toughen our spiritual fiber. We cannot surmount or remove them of ourselves, but God makes "a way" for us to pass through them, even as he cleared the way for the children of Israel to cross the Red Sea in their desperate flight from their pursuers. The mountains will become a way through which we can pass if that is the road the Lord would have us take.

Let us be glad for the mountains in our lives— glad for the vast reaches, the glory to be attained at the summits, the far vision that is ours after the long, arduous climb. Let us be glad for the obstacles that will make us stronger in our going. Let us be glad for a God who makes his mountains a way for his otherwise helpless children.

He wants us to attain to the high pinnacles of earth that we may have a broader view of life as he desires us to live it, and he wants us to have a better conception of his part in our living.

It must please him mightily when he sees his children climbing homeward with unfaltering trust and with high courage, with always a living, shining faith burning like a steady flame in their hearts. He doeth all things well. Let us trust him!

Yonder the blue horizon;
　Yonder the upward climb,
With the mountains in the distance
　That we shall reach in time,
God going ahead to open
　A safe way for our feet,
As safe as any worn road
　Or any traveled street.
Whatever our destination,
　Whatever may be our day,
The mountains that lie before us
　Will have become a way
To grander and vaster summits
　Than any we yet have found.
Climb upward, onward, comrades,
　To reach that higher ground.

Thou knowest, Lord God, our feeble frames. Thou rememberest that we are dust. Our dependence is solely upon thee. Make the way plain before our feet. Give us victory in seeming defeat. Help us to grow strong in thy strength that we may reach the far heights which thou desirest us to reach. We ask it in Christ's name. Amen.

14

"What Is That in Thine Hand?"

And the Lord said unto him, What is that in thine hand? And he said, A rod. And he said, Cast it on the ground. . . . And it became a serpent.
—Exod. 4:2-3

And the Lord said unto Moses, Wherefore criest thou unto me? speak unto the children of Israel, that they go forward: but lift thou up thy rod, and stretch out thine hand over the sea, and divide it: and the children of Israel shall go on dry ground through the midst of the sea.   —Exod. 14:15-16

TWICE OF old a commonplace thing within a man's hand was used to glorify God. Doubtless the rod Moses carried was a simple shepherd's crook, which goes to prove that the plainest thing may become an instrument of service for our Lord.

Once Moses' rod was used to show God's power through a strange miracle; it became a serpent at God's command. Another time it was the vital instrument that caused the Red Sea to divide so that a great throng of anxious, hurrying people might pass safely over on their historical journey to the Promised Land.

If such a simple thing in a man's hand proved to be thus important, why should not the everyday utensils in women's hands bring about some modern miracle?

One lesson to be learned here is evident: the Lord rebuked Moses for crying to him to do the work that Moses himself could do. He had that within his hand which would serve the purpose, and God is ever desirous that we should be self-reliant and helpful in his service.

What have we in our hands today? What have you in yours? What have I in mine? These are vital questions, and we must answer them wisely and well. Is it a Bible, perhaps, that must be conned long and earnestly if we are to teach others its important and life-giving truths? Is it a pen with which one may set her heart down in poetry or music to bless the world? Is it a brush out of which may flow color so vivid that the work may last for centuries as a contribution to beauty itself? Is it a needle, that glistening small instrument used by women throughout the centuries to bring cheer and comfort to the members of their households? Is it a dust mop, a flour sifter, a dishrag, a tea towel? These too add to the graciousness of home-sweet living and are pleasing in the Lord's sight, for was it not he who established homes and placed families therein from the beginning?

What is that in your hand? Is it a child's hand —the child God has given you? This without question is the greatest responsibility entrusted to womankind—that little hand held tightly within your own! Oh, may we value that trust as we should!

Is there perhaps a hand in yours of some sorrowing one who has reached out to you in her need for understanding sympathy? Truly this is a charge which we should not fail to hold as sacred.

The hands of upright Christian women are ever filled with good works. God grant that we as church workers, as home keepers, as teachers, as businesswomen, keep them thus filled by remembering that all things can and should be used to the glory of God. All womanly activities are pleasing to him, of this we may be very sure.

One dear old mother at the sunset of her life confided in her friend thus: "I know my time is limited here upon earth, and I often fall to wondering if I am really fit to meet my Master. Why, all I have ever done was to rear my children to the best of my ability and to keep my home a cheerful and happy place for them. I have had no extra strength for outside work at all," and she sighed over what she considered her lack. The friend was quick to remind her of the great work her children were doing out in the world. One was a minister, one a missionary, one a noted physician—all Christians and doing service for their Master, which was the fruit of the seed planted by that devoted mother long ago.

What is that in your hand? Let us scan each commonplace article in everyday use and see in it the rod of Moses made serviceable through God's willingness to accept it.

God gives each one some special thing to do
    To further his great kingdom on the earth.
What is within your hand the long day through
    To shape into some vital thing of worth
For God's own glory and for your own soul's
    good,
    For the good of others as you travel on?
What craft, what splendid art is yours that would
    Make life the richer before day is done?

Perhaps it may be but the gentle art
    Of being kind to others in their need,
A faculty for easing some hurt heart
    Or eyes to see or listening ears to heed
The constant cry for help from land to land.
What is it, O my comrade, in your hand?

Our heavenly Father, we would be wise in our everyday living. We would consider no day commonplace, no plain task beneath us, no implement without its worth, since all things that thou hast made are honorable and good.

We would not be weary in well-doing, for we are told that in due season we shall reap if we faint not. We open our hands in thy sight. Help us to use what they hold for thy glory. In Christ's name we ask it. Amen.

Vision

Where there is no vision, the people perish.
—Prov. 29:18

And the word of the Lord was precious in those days; there was no open vision. —I Sam. 3:1

TRULY IT must have been a privilege to live in the days when God revealed his purposes toward men through direct contact, when angels were entertained at tent doors or wherever they appeared with their vital messages to certain ones for whom God had special plans.

In the days of the open vision we may be assured that he wanted men to take the far look, the look that takes in the things of eternity. He wanted them to take their eyes from the minute details of every day and look at him and to him in order that they might discover his purpose in their lives.

Too often we keep our eyes on the road and not on the beautiful distances ahead that hold the hope of a brighter and better tomorrow. We are like the man who could look no way but down and therefore saw only the muck of the road, and he missed the shining and colorful glory of the rainbow after the storm.

There is an incident told of a busy woman who had gone to an oculist for help for an eye trouble. The doctor made every possible test, and at last he leaned back in his chair and surveyed his patient thoughtfully.

"Is there a beautiful view anywhere near your house?" he asked.

For a moment the woman stared at him, amazed at such a question. Then she thought that possibly he was tired and might be wanting to relax a while before further examination, and she answered, "Yes, there is a lovely view across the distant hills from one of our upstairs windows. The country is nice at this time of year, isn't it?"

The doctor ignored the last remark. "How often do you look at those hills?"

"Why, every day or two, I suppose. You see, that view is out beyond our guest-room windows, and I'm not in there very often."

"And when you do look out of that window, how much time do you give to that view?"

"Oh, perhaps a minute," she said, beginning to be a bit annoyed at the persistent questioning.

"And yet it is a beautiful view?" the doctor was quizzical.

"Yes, it is," she said, "but I am a very busy woman. There are many demands being made upon my time. I do all the sewing for my family, all the cooking and dishwashing, the laundry and the ironing. A housewife hasn't much time for mere scenery. I have to use my eyes for close work most of the time."

"And that's exactly what tires them," said the doctor, rising. "If you wish to care for those eyes of yours, make an ironclad rule to gaze at that beautiful distant view for at least twenty minutes of the day—longer if possible. Keep your eyes wide open. Study the contour of those hills. Watch the changing colors over them. Take the far look often, if you know what I mean. If you keep it up, you won't need to come to me again for a long while, if ever."

The woman told the story months later to friends, and in answer to their questioning she said delightedly, "Yes, I followed his advice, and it worked; all that my tired eyes needed was the rest of what he called the far look. I wonder," she added thoughtfully, "if the wise doctor knew for how much more than weary eyes he was prescribing? My soul needed to be stretched as well as my vision. My body needed to lose its tension, and the recreation gained was miraculous. The twenty minutes soon grew into an hour, and it became the most important part of my day. Instinctively as I gazed out over those peaceful,

lovely hills, my mental eyes began to take note
of the important things of life. The little cares
close at hand seemed to slip away, and they no
longer were of much moment. I could see farther
into the future and higher in the scale of values;
my mental eyesight grew stronger and clearer
along with the physical. It is possible, I am sure,"
she added, "to have eyestrain of the soul as well
as of the body. Oh yes, the practice is far too
valuable to let go, and I keep on seeking my
window for the rich reward it gives me."

So shall we not, too, seek some window that
faces toward the dawn where God lights his fires
of hope for the day, or a window that looks westward where the glowing embers die in great
glory, and shall we not take the far look at things
eternal with their limitless possibilities? Shall we
not look until we see God back of the purpose in
our lives and then go forward strengthened for
the day's work? Is this not what he wants us to
do? I believe it is.

Open our eyes, dear Lord, that we may see
The far vast reaches of eternity.
Help us to look beyond life's little cares
So prone to fret us and the grief that wears
Our courage thin. Oh, may we tune our hearts
To thy great harmony, that all the parts
May ever be in perfect sweet accord.
Give us thy own clear vision, blessed Lord.

Our heavenly Father, we would stretch our sight until the important things of life take their rightful places in our living. We would take the far look that turns our vision toward thee, and thus we would see thy will concerning us and accept it gladly.

May we be wise to discover the beauty of thy handiwork and to worship thee as we should for all thy marvelous gifts to us. Amen.

16

Prayer

Pray without ceasing. —I Thess. 5:17

Be careful for nothing; but in every thing by prayer and supplication with thanksgiving let your requests be made known unto God. —Phil. 4:6

THROUGHOUT the ages prayers have gone up to the throne of God, taking their sure and certain way, there to draw upon the inexhaustible resources of the almighty Father of humanity.

Prayers are still rising ceaselessly every moment of every hour of every day and will continue to rise until the last man stands upon the shores of eternity, so great is our need for a higher and more sustaining power than lies within ourselves.

There are prayers that clutch at the very robes of God. They are like hands beating against his breast as hurt hearts cry out in an agony of supplication. There are the prayers of the sorrowing who turn to God for help in their overwhelming bereavement. There are the lighthearted voicings of those who are glad with the joy of living. There are the prayers of the patient ones of earth who pray, and continue to pray, ever aware of God beyond unanswered prayer. There are the pleading voices of the weary, importuning God for rest when the burdens of life grow too heavy for their tired shoulders to bear. There are the prayers of the craven, those cowardly ones who turn to God only when sudden fear for their own welfare drives them to their knees.

Alas! far and away the importuning prayers outnumber those of praise and thanksgiving. Truly this is a sad commentary upon human behavior. We plead; we beg; we cry aloud; but often we neglect the prayers of gratitude due a kind and loving Father.

These would be the prayers that are the most pleasing to him. His mercies are all about us, and for these our voices should ever lift in sincere and heartfelt praise.

The whole troubled world today is seeking for one who understands our inner needs. Prayer too often becomes a clamorous thing. We do all the talking. We do not listen enough. We fail to await the answer. Far too many times we do not expect it. If we would only "study to be quiet," to "be still, and know that [he is] God," even as he has told us thus to do, out of that silence would come his answer clear and plain. His voice would speak peace to our troubled hearts, and we would find the rest we so crave.

Why do we not accord him the same courtesy we give to our earthly friends in our conversation with them? Would it not be rude indeed if we never gave them the opportunity to answer our petitionings, if such there be? Would it not truly be strange?

If he were not the patient God that he is, he surely would close his ears to the noisy confusion of our cries; but we know that his loving heart will never permit him to do so. "Before they call, I will answer," God says through the prophet Isaiah. "Your Father knoweth what things ye have need of," Christ says. God knows even as a true mother knows the needs of her earthly children before they speak. She answers that need, and so does God. Why should we doubt his ability and willingness to do so? Every child is individual unto himself. God knows this and why we are motivated as we are; and he loves us, he forgives our shortcomings, and he answers our prayers for our good in his own wise and certain way.

Oh, that we might more often "praise the Lord for his goodness, and for his wonderful works to the children of men"!

The privilege of prayer! How amazing it is that

we are permitted to approach an almighty **God** with our simple everyday problems and desires! And more amazing still is the fact that he has bidden us come to him in prayer and that he answers those prayers always in one way or another.

We are taught by our Lord how to pray. His prayer encompasses the whole of living. His is selfless prayer while we too often are inclined to pray for our own alone, for "me and mine" and not for a world that is struggling in want and darkness, greatly in need of our earnest interest and our prayers. He wants us to reach out to all peoples, all nations. His first thought is for God's kingdom that is to come here upon the earth. He bids us pray for this. He bids us pray that God's will be done here as well as in heaven. He tells us to pray for bread—for our daily bread, not for my bread alone. Surely all Christians should think beyond their own small circle to the great circle that includes the whole wide world.

God's will and his interest should be our will and our interest. May we be willing co-workers with him as we pray. Let us be listeners as well as supplicants. Let us strive more earnestly to please our heavenly Father in our praying even as good and obedient children strive to please their earthly parents as they ask favors of them and with grateful hearts give thanks for those favors. Let

us heed our Lord's words, "Pray without ceasing,
for our need is great.

What would we do if it were not for prayer?
   The human heart has desperate need of God,
Whether it be in joy or deep despair,
   Or if we faint beneath some chastening rod.
We come, we kneel, and there close at his feet
We find his comfort, and we find it sweet.

What would we do if there were none to hear
   Our clear-voiced praise, our hurt cry of distress?
What would we do without our Lord when fear
   Or pain be ours, and he should fail to bless
The seeking one down paths that have grown
      dim?
What would we do if it were not for him?

Our heavenly Father, we come humbly to thee,
knowing our unworthiness and our utter dependence upon thee. We realize our faults and our failures, and how often our prayers are remiss. Help us
to be overcomers. Help us to be pleasing in thy sight
as thy children.

Grant that we may pray aright at all times. May
we make our petitions known unto thee through
prayer with thanksgiving, that the peace which
passeth all understanding may keep our minds and
hearts through Jesus Christ our Lord. Amen.

17

Faith

Now faith is the substance of things hoped for, the evidence of things not seen.   —Heb. 11:1

FAITH is a living, shining thing in the heart of a believer. It gleams there like bright sunlight gleaming upon new silver. It is not an ephemeral mist. It is a substance, we are told—the substance of things hoped for. It is the evidence of things that our eyes have not seen, but which our spirits are aware of and acquainted with.

Say the word, and it holds within its meaning something of the glory that the brave of earth have ever known in their forward march. There is a singing through it. We listen, and we hear countless thousands of clear voices lifting in the old familiar hymn, "Faith of Our Fathers," and we find our own hearts strengthened as we recall the stalwart and unfaltering faith that was theirs through stress and storm, through sunshine and shadow.

Faith holds within itself the healing for hurts that mankind long has borne. We cannot describe faith, yet it abides with all who are willing to be thus companioned. We cannot touch it, yet it holds the hands of those who reach out for it, and it will guide any traveler safely on the way.

We need never lose it, whether our journey be by sea or land. With its high torch to light the alien skies we can face life and death fearlessly, for we know in whom we have believed. We know that he is able to keep that which we have committed unto him—our lives, our bodies, our souls—for all eternity.

Faith is a power beyond all conception. It brings the believer pardon, freedom, oneness with Christ, victory through Christ, heirship, and eternal life. And "all things, whatsoever ye shall ask in prayer, believing, ye shall receive."

It enables the believer to stand, to walk, to fight, to overcome. It makes one of unfaltering faith accepted, justified, sanctified. It brings its own reward in the form of the bread of life, the living water, peace, power, righteousness, and redemption. There are references in our Bibles to prove all this. Faith, that thing of glory, has for its synonyms things of power and of might.

Christ evaluated faith when he said, "If ye have faith as a grain of mustard seed, ye shall say unto this mountain, Remove hence to yonder place; and it shall remove; and nothing shall be impossible unto you." Oh, the marvelous power of faith! Think of it—*nothing*, Christ said, shall be impossible! What an astonishing statement! And how important it is that we strive daily to increase our faith!

What mighty works the Christian can accomplish with even a little faith! The mustard-seed size can do wonders, but what could a full working faith accomplish? The mountains of sin in lives and the gigantic obstacles that obstruct the way to righteous living would immediately vanish, and the eternal verities would stand before us like bright landmarks to point the way to heaven.

What world-shaking events would take place if every professing Christian moved forward with unshakable and growing faith in almighty God! Would we not take on something of his attributes with that power working within us? And would he not rejoice to have us as his co-workers?

In one place Christ says that "men ought always to pray and not to faint," and further on he says sorrowfully, "When the Son of man cometh, shall he find faith on the earth?" Oh, the pity of it that he, taking the long look, should have reason to question thus! We look about us today at all the wild clamor of our time and see what he saw centuries ago: the great lack of working faith even in the churches of the day, the indifference to Christ's teachings with the world being too much with us. He could look ahead and see the "whited sepulchres, which indeed appear beautiful outward, but are within full of dead men's bones." God grant we may awaken to the serious situation of the world today.

How are we to increase our faith? How can we help others build a firmer foundation for Christian living? We are told that "faith cometh by hearing, and hearing by the word of God." Thus again we have the admonition to turn often to God's Word for knowledge and wisdom. Thus only can we give out the word so that others may hear it, and the "substance" and the "evidence" of faith may spring up in their hearts from the seeds we have planted.

Christ was ever acutely aware of the thing called faith. He recognized it gladly when those with whom he came in contact possessed it. "I have not found so great faith, no, not in Israel." "O woman, great is thy faith." "Thy faith hath made thee whole." Over and over he expressed his approbation of one with a living faith. May he be able to do so with us.

"How is it that ye have no faith?" once he questioned gravely. The Word points out that faith in Christ is essential to salvation. None can come to the Father save through his Son Jesus Christ, and without faith in that Son none can be saved.

Let us also remember that the Word says "faith, if it hath not works, is dead." Paul said, "Though I have all faith, so that I could remove mountains, and have not charity, I am nothing." Therefore let us have faith. Let us work diligently, for truly the night cometh when no one can work, and let us have a working charity for our kind lest we become as "sounding brass, or a tinkling cymbal." Jesus faith was so great that nothing was impossible for him.

Nothing was too great for him to do
When faith shone like clear sunlight in men's
eyes.
That faith was his high challenge, and he knew
Their need and answered all their heartfelt
cries.
He must have watched and waited for that sign—
The light of hope, the faith that did not dim—
Before he gave his tender and divine
Healing to the ones who came to him.

Lord, I would tend the lamp within my heart,
The lighted lamp held high for you to see;
All I need is faith to do my part,
And you will do the rest, the best for me.
Behold my faith, dear Lord, and may it bring
The solace of your blessed comforting.

Our heavenly Father, help us so to strengthen our faith that we may come to thee assured of thy approbation and thy blessing. We do not want to be deserving of thy sorrowful rebuke because of our lack of faith. We believe in thee, we love thee, and we trust thee.

May we ever work to please thee with a strong and shining faith glowing in our hearts. Help us to keep remembering that nothing is impossible to those who believe. We ask most earnestly for wisdom and strength at all times to lay hold of the glory that awaits all with faith enough to receive it. Amen.

18

Fortification

The Lord thy God in the midst of thee is mighty.
—Zeph. 3:17

IF WE often feel that our strength and capabilities are inadequate for the work we have set ourselves to do for our Lord, if we falter weakly and consider ourselves unworthy of the faith God has in us, let us go to his Word for his proffered strength which he holds out to us freely and ungrudgingly.

In our seeking we will come across these important and consequential words, "The Lord thy God in the midst of thee is mighty." If we pause to consider them as we should, we can straighten and grow strong at once. We become fortified as with steel, for the power and the might of God begins working in us with its unfailing strength.

None need be weak with that inherent strength moving within. We need only to take hold of it. If we do so, we need not fail in any righteous endeavor, and none need fear failure. Fear, we realize, is the worm that gnaws at the core of life to hurt and destroy our confidence in ourselves. It blocks our faith, that shining thing of the spirit so necessary to true and upright Christian living.

Why should any heart fear with the might of God in its midst? When we are weak, then are we strong—not in our own strength but in his, and he will enable us to go forward in that strength.

It is reasonable to believe that he who left his unfinished work with his followers is concerned about that work, and he will help us accomplish each far-reaching and important task. It must be done, and it will be done, for he will see that it is done.

There is much said of a Christian's faith in God, but there is little told of the faith he has in mankind. There is an old and beautiful legend that tells of that far-off day of the Ascension when Jesus stepped upon the shores of heaven. It tells of the angels running to meet him with eager questioning as to his stay upon earth.

"Did you finish your work?" they asked.

"No," Jesus replied, "it is not finished."

"But if it is not finished, who then will do it?"

"I left the work with my disciples," he told them.

"But what if they fail?" they persisted anxious-

ly, and Jesus, moving forward, answered simply,
"They will not fail."

Oh, to think that he has such unwavering
faith, such real need of us, his followers! He is
confident that his work will go forward, and we
cannot, dare not, fail him.

We cannot do his work without his strength
within us, mighty and unfailing. We should
never grow discouraged or fearful in any righteous
undertaking. Let us remember that the Lord has
confidence in us because his might is working in
us. He has absolute faith that we will go forward
to bring about his kingdom upon the earth.

"The Lord thy God in the midst of thee is
mighty." Let us fix the words forever upon our
hearts, for in all God's promises there is no more
assuring statement, no more soul-strengthening
word than this. Let us lay hold upon it and thus
meet every issue of life, every task to be done,
with high courage and unwavering faith.

"The Lord thy God in the midst of thee is
    mighty."
We say the words; we reach our hands to claim
The bright fulfillment of his blessed promise
    That comforts, cheers, and warms our hearts
    like flame.
We are fortified and strengthened for our labor;
    We straighten as the burdens roll away;
We have thy promise, blessed Lord and Master,

That the strength thou givest will be as our day,
And thou art in our midst. We cannot fail thee
Whatever task be ours, O blessed Lord.
Thy strength shall be our strength, thy power our
power;
We cling to this, thine own unfailing word.

Our Lord God, we thy disciples would be unfaltering followers of thee and thy Son Jesus Christ.
We thank thee for thy faith in us thy children. We
thank thee for the assurance of thy aid at all times
and for the confidence it gives us in our work. May
thy kingdom truly come, and may we be worthy
helpers in bringing it about. We ask it in Jesus'
name. Amen.

19

Stewardship

Let a man so account of us, as of the ministers
of Christ, and stewards of the mysteries of God.
Moreover it is required in stewards, that a man be
found faithful.   —I Cor. 4:1-2

ONE IS inclined to think of stewardship as simply
the tithing of one's income, forgetting its full and
vital significance which is the stewardship of life
itself—the stewardship of our time, our strength,
our love, our hope, and our courage, and of comfort to be meted out to others in their need.

To be ministers of Christ is a high and sacred
calling; to be stewards of the mysteries of God is
a responsibility and a privilege beyond anything
that the heart could ask or think. We should be
humble before this trust, and we should be proud
to be thus chosen.

There is a requirement, as there ever is in

positions of great responsibility. We are told we must be faithful in our outgiving. A faithless steward is a worthless one. To be faithful means we are to keep books for God with his just and righteous share held out for him. It means praying to be guided in the use of these funds, that we may be wise in dispensing them as we are with our own. It means faithfulness in the giving of ourselves to the work of the kingdom.

As God looks down upon us today, he must be immeasurably pleased with many who have not faltered or failed in their labor for him. These are the ones who are constantly going about doing good, even as did our Lord while he was here upon earth. He makes note of those who serve faithfully even in the humblest capacity as well as of those who serve in high places. He approves of all who put his work first.

He looks upon the heart and knows every effort that the faithful are making in his behalf, and his "Well done, good and faithful servant," will be ample reward. Alas! he knows also who are the unfaithful stewards. He has much to say of them in his Word. They were called severely to account, even as we shall be if we fail to do the work entrusted to us.

To some he has given five talents, to others two, to others one. He does not expect as great returns from the smaller amounts, but he does expect a true report even from these. From those to whom he has given much he expects much. Make no mistake about that. Oh, may we be faithful!

We are told, "The Lord thy God is a jealous God." Would he not be jealous of our time? Does he not want us to use it for his glory? Think of the many wasted hours through our days. Surely he is cognizant of every moment we employ in his service, and also he is clearly aware of the time we so often fritter away in self-indulgence and in gainless employment.

Let us be more consistent in our Christian living. Let us put first things first—those eternal things of God. If we are spiritually gifted to cheer and comfort others, are we not stewards of a blessed commodity? Should we not mete it out unsparingly? If we can lift the burden from shoulders overburdened, is it not a part of our stewardship to share with the weaker ones the strength that God has given us?

God loaned me life, and I must pay
Him back a portion of each day
In loving service; I must give
A part of every hour I live
In thoughtful, kindly deeds to others
Who are my sisters and my brothers.

God loaned me coins I may not spend
For any wasteful, selfish end.
They are a trust that I must hold
As sacred. All the world's bright gold
Belongs to him, and in my spending
I must repay his gracious lending.

God put his love within my heart,
A love I ever must impart
To a world in desperate need of care.
All things God gives me I must share.
This is the stewardship of living,
A spontaneous and joyous giving.

Our dear heavenly Father, we would be thy faithful stewards. Give us, we pray, the clear insight into thy mysteries that we may be aware of the debt we owe thee. And may we pay it in full.

We thank thee for our various talents. We would return them to thee greatly amplified. Help us that we may be bearers of fruit for thy heavenly kingdom. This we ask in the name of Jesus thy Son. Amen.

20

The Ancient Landmarks

Remove not the ancient landmark, which thy fathers have set. —Prov. 22:28

Thou shalt not remove thy neighbour's landmark, which they of old time have set in thine inheritance, which thou shalt inherit in the land that the Lord thy God giveth thee to possess it.
—Deut. 19:14

IN CONNING these verses one wonders if the two which are so widely separated in God's Word are not after all closely related and linked together for our enlightenment.

The ancient landmarks may well be translated as "faith of our fathers"—a working faith that established many directing signs along our way that should never under any circumstance be destroyed. Their faith was founded upon the rock of Jesus Christ, and nothing on earth can shake it, neither earthquake nor hurricane, neither doubt nor disaster. The work established through that faith has become a lamp to our feet and a guide to our pathway.

Oh, may we never remove it! Should we do so, myriads would lose their way and go wandering afar in dire confusion. Too often we hear words uttered that are like wedges being driven in to pry loose the old landmarks. There are subtle teachings that would, if it were possible, shatter the granite of the Word of God. There are antichrists who would crash their way over and through those staying bars, ignoring them, denying that they exist; but the true believer stands firm in reverence before them, endeavoring to learn more of that which they stand for and to understand the root and strength of those long established rules and laws.

He who adds to or takes away from the Word of God should beware. He whose teaching is false should flee from the wrath of a just and righteous God.

There is much that is ugly in modern art, much that is beautiful; but when the ugliness entirely overshadows the beauty, then the so-called art will be on its way out, as it should be. When one's teaching is not based on truth, God will see to it that its falseness shall vanish from the earth, and truth and beauty will supplant it.

"Thou shalt not remove thy neighbour's landmark," which is his inheritance. Does this not sound a warning to false doctrines? Is it not a grave evil to strive to undermine another's faith, his firm-grounded belief? Woe to the one who attempts to do this evil thing! God will have none of it!

There is so much magnificence, such certainty and steadfast assurance in the true Word of God that none should wander afar seeking to alter its meaning. When he does so, he brings back nothing but ashes in his hands to offer to thirsty, seeking souls. God grant we may drink so deeply of the Living Water that we may have words to speak that will be thirst quenching and life sustaining.

Is it not well to keep in remembrance the ancient landmarks that are not to be torn down? May we never remove them. May we never destroy by word or deed our neighbors' guards that are their inheritance from their righteous forebears. This would be sin indeed.

Lord God, we thank thee for the warnings given us throughout thy Word. Without them we would climb roughshod over the protecting barriers set up by our Christian fathers. Give us understanding, that we may not tear down when we should build up, that we may never injure another by the voicing of a false belief. Truly help us, Lord, that we may ever live according to thy will. Amen.

21

Whosoever

And it shall come to pass, that whosoever shall call on the name of the Lord shall be delivered.
—Joel 2:32

"WHOSOEVER"—the word is all-encompassing. It means every human being on earth. It means the heathen as well as the Christian. It means the millions who make up the different races of the earth, for in God's sight there is no distinction whatsoever.

It means you, and it means me. "Whosoever shall call on the name of the Lord *shall* be delivered!" One could write the sentence over with the different words italicized for emphasis, and the thought would remain strong; yet the plain and simple statement is emphasis enough to make us all conscious of its far-reaching significance.

"*Shall* be delivered"—delivered from what? Delivered from sin and the bondage of sin; de-

livered from evil and the awful consequences of
evil. It means what it says. The part we are to
have in its bearing on humanity is to take or to
send the blessed news to the farthest corners of
the earth, that it may be spread abroad until
the last man and woman and child shall be in-
formed of the everlasting mercies of the Lord
our God.

How can anyone who does not know of God
and his saving grace know how to "call"? And
how can he be delivered unless he calls?

He must be told that there is a God who has
promised deliverance to everyone who will call
upon his name. He must be told that he will
have the certain and sure reward offered in that
promise. What hope it will bring to the seeking
and troubled heart! What joy will be in the
fulfillment of the promise!

Without doubt there are countless baffled and
bewildered souls who have clung to this special
promise. Many of them may be the simple ones
of earth who dare not so much as lift their eyes
to heaven, as is told of the publican of old, but
they dare draw hope and courage from this all-
encompassing and significant promise. There
must ever have been many who in hours of temptation and suffering have prayed desperately for
release, and who have suddenly come upon this
wonderful promise and there found strength and

comfort to go forward. Doubtless it has acted as a healing medicine in their lives, renewing their hope for deliverance and strengthening their faith that had grown dim and faltering.

We who know of God and his saving power are bound by a great and grave responsibility. We must not shirk that responsibility. We must tell it out—tell that the Lord is no respecter of persons, that he is willing and able to save to the uttermost the poorest on earth or those who fare sumptuously. His "whosoever" is a challenge that we all can meet.

"Then shalt thou call, and the Lord shall answer." There is to be no delay as to his hearing our cries, and the answer will come in his own good time, and that time is always the right time. Our place is to call and to teach others to find their own tongues in prayer and supplication.

Surely there is no greater work for any woman than this. Surely there is nothing that pleases God more than to see the efforts being made for the evangelization of the whole world. Surely this is what he bade us do that bright spring day before his ascension into heaven. Let us be quick to heed his command.

"Whosoever"—oh, the blessed word!
　　It glows across the centuries like flame.

Hark, it is his voice; thus saith the Lord:
  "Whosoever shall call upon my name
Shall be delivered." Lord, my need is great,
    The night is dark, the hills ahead are steep,
But I have called, dear Lord, and I can wait
    The promise which I know that thou wilt
      keep.

The promise made to all earth's creeds and
      kinds,
  For every race of men beneath the sun.
Thy "whosoever" is a link that binds
  Us all together and that makes us one.
Thou wilt deliver all who call on thee.
    My friends, that promise holds for you and
      me.

Our heavenly Father, we would not fail to call
upon thee in our great need. We would not doubt
that deliverance will come from thee in answer to
our call. We would trust thee at all times, and,
Lord God, we would ever be mindful of the soul
need of others. We would be diligent in spreading
thy word abroad that they may learn of thee. Help
us as we pray; we ask it in thy Son Jesus' name.
Amen.

22

The High Calling

Brethren, I count not myself to have apprehended but this one thing I do, forgetting those things which are behind, and reaching forth unto those things which are before, I press toward the mark for the prize of the high calling of God in Christ Jesus. —Phil. 3:13-14

"THE PRIZE of the high calling of God." Reaching for it and pressing toward the mark to gain it— what a sense of determined action the picture presents! And what a blessed course to pursue!

To press forward toward the prize, which surely means the salvation of the soul, that reward which God calls us by Christ Jesus to receive. Surely it is a prize worth striving for.

Paul was particularly wise when he spoke of "forgetting those things which are behind." He would have been greatly handicapped in his forward progress had he kept regretfully remembering his past. Strange that he should have believed while "breathing out threatenings and slaughter," and even while sanctioning murder, that he was doing God's service. It is good that he could forget even as God forgets as he forgives our sins.

Therefore he was able to put all his efforts into concentrating upon his one great purpose, the pressing forward toward the mark of the prize held out to him in the hand of God.

We too would be wise to forget the past with its shortcomings and failures as we move toward the great fulfillment of our lives. God through Jesus is waiting to give that prize to all who will accept it. May we not fail to do our part.

Paul was unusually humble. He did not claim to be aware of all the deep meaning of the Word, but he knew what he was seeking and went after it with unfaltering determination.

We may not be wise enough to comprehend at once all the heights and depths of meaning in God's Word, but there is none who cannot strive to understand. We may be sure the meaning will be revealed to every earnest seeker after the truth. God did not make his plan of salvation an enigma impossible of solution. He makes the way plain, and he wants us to study the Word as a child cons his books; then he wants us to clarify it as it is revealed to us, that others may more readily come to know the one true and living God.

We recall the humble man of Ethiopia as he sat in his chariot earnestly reading Isaiah the prophet. We note how Philip ran to be of help and questioned, "Understandest thou what thou readest?" And then came the strangely pathetic and wistful answer, "How can I, except some man should guide me?"

What a truly great occasion was the conversion and baptism in the river that ran brightly that beautiful spring day.

To bring even one soul to Christ is worth a lifetime of endeavor. We are told that those who receive the truth become the "city of the living God" and the "temple of the most High." What architects any who go seeking to save souls may become!

The white fields are waiting. Every loyal follower of the Christ should be his husbandman, ready to go forth to the reaping and to bear the precious sheaves to the Master. Should we not want to be sharing the salvation that is ours through the unmerited favor of our Lord and Saviour Jesus Christ?

Let us press forward with our eyes on the Christ, yet let us not be so self-centered that we forget to cry out to others on the way, "Come, each and every one. Press forward toward the

prize of the high calling of God in Jesus Christ."
This will be true sharing of the salvation he is
offering to us all.

"Cry aloud, spare not, lift up thy voice,"
    Trumpet-clear there comes the grave com-
        mand.
"Shew my people their transgression"; bid
    Them turn from evil ways and firmly stand
Upon the rock which is the Christ our Lord.
Cry aloud the all-important word.

May no wayfaring traveler lose his way
    For lack of warning. Pitfalls lie ahead,
And we are bid to stay our headlong flight.
    "Cry aloud, spare not," the prophet said.
Lord, help us reach a firm detaining hand,
    And may we lift clear voices in the crowd
To help all wanderers in a darkened land
    And draw them to thee as we cry aloud.

Lord God, we would press forward toward the
prize of thy high calling. We would forget the past,
remembering that it would only hinder us in our
forward going. We would cry aloud the message
of thy salvation, that others may turn and face
toward the light of thy glory and thus be saved.
Help us at all times, dear Lord, to do thy blessed
will, knowing that it will always be safe and good
and right for us to do so. Amen.

23

The Ministry of Service

For he hath regarded the low estate of his hand-maiden: for, behold, from henceforth all generations shall call me blessed.   —Luke 1:48

THERE is an old story, universally beloved, beginning thus: "And it came to pass in those days, that there went out a decree from Caesar Augustus, that all the world should be taxed. . . . And Joseph also went up from Galilee, out of the city of Nazareth, . . . unto . . . Bethlehem, . . . to be taxed with Mary his espoused wife."

Evidently taxes were as great a problem in those days as they have been since. One can well get the picture of those two in the little Nazareth home. If it was then as it is today, Joseph must have bent above his accounts, making note of the number of tools and implements of his trade, summing up honestly the profits from the sale of his hand-hewn yokes and tables and chairs, setting aside carefully the amount to

107

be rendered unto Caesar. The sweet-faced Mary must have stood near by, now and then offering some helpful suggestion which pleased him.

Then came the day for their departure to Bethlehem. I love to picture the little household early astir that there need be no haste, for there was grave reason why Mary should go slowly on the journey.

I can see them going down the winding hill road in the sparkling, frosty morning, Joseph and the woman he loved. She riding, he guiding the gentle beast with now and then a word. I am sure they must have stopped to rest at noontime beneath some old brooding tree, its branches bereft of foliage yet it was still a gracious resting place for these two. They must have supped gratefully of wine from an earthen jug and have broken gladly their wholesome brown-crusted loaf.

In the early twilight, because the way had been long, they came wearily down the twisting cobblestone streets of a village to an inn overfull. One can see Joseph helping his beloved to alight, guarding her lest she stumble on the loose cobblestones, gazing at her with anxious eyes to ascertain whether the journey had proved too great for her strength.

Then at last there was the stable, filled with the fragrance of meadow hay and warm from the breath and the bodies of the housed oxen. Here was the peace that the woman needed, away from the clamor and din of the stable yard with its noisy incoming and outgoing guests, away from the stir and flutter of beasts and doves waiting the morning sacrifice.

Then in this sweet seclusion Mary made ready for rest. One can see her kneeling at the manger-side thanking Jehovah for their safe arrival and for the humble shelter for the night, her face taking on an ethereal light from the star dust that filtered through the rafters above.

Then as she arose, suddenly she knew her hour had come—the great hour when she, a humble woman, was to bear the Saviour of the world.

Surely there was some good woman in the neighborhood who would come to help her. Joseph doubtless went hurriedly seeking such a one—a woman with the inherent knowledge of women at such a time as this, one who could minister to her kind in need, a woman with the God-given capability to meet a crisis ably.

Thus this unknown, unsung woman was the first to minister to the little Lord's bodily needs. The swaddling clothes were not stable equipment. Doubtless they had been washed and made sweet with sun and wind, and laid away in a cedar-scented chest for some future need.

The winding of those garments could only have been executed by hands familiar with the task.

This was womankind's first service for our Lord. How countless and valued were those ministrations in his latter life! How vital they were to his well-being! Mary's ministry began that night and lasted for thirty-three years, years that must have been exquisite with joy and pain and sorrow. What a privilege and blessing was hers!

Her exemplary motherhood is a beacon light for all mothers. Oh, that each woman who bears a child would set one goal before her eyes, praying that her child may take on something of the white purity of the Christ, something of his wisdom and clean strength, making that prayer a determination on her part to lead that child with God's help into a life of righteousness.

Today, because of that far night, in the countless small homes of earth mothers everywhere are doing the simple, beautiful things that gladden children's hearts as they recall that other mother and the Child of long ago who still awaits and gladly receives the treasures of the spirit we can bring to him and whatever material gifts we can give to his lowly ones of earth who have need of cheer and beauty and brightness in lives that otherwise might be dull.

Our heavenly Father, thou didst honor one of our kind with an honor so great we stand in awe before it. May we take on something of her beauty of character, something of the purity of her life, that we too may be blessed by the nearness of her Son Jesus Christ in our daily living.

We thank thee for Mary, the mother of our Lord. All history would be dimmed without her fragile beauty, her steadfastness, and her grace. Help us to be women after thine own heart, we pray. Amen.

24

Motherhood's Greatest Gift

And she vowed a vow, and said, O Lord of hosts, if thou wilt indeed look on the affliction of thine handmaid, and remember me, and not forget thine handmaid, but wilt give unto thine handmaid a man child, then I will give him unto the Lord all the days of his life.   —I Sam. 1:11

VIVID is the picture of Hannah—sorrowful of spirit, kneeling in the house of the Lord and praying that God would grant her the desire of her heart. That desire was that she might have the child for whom she had prayed and had waited for so long.

We can see her kneeling as she "spake in her heart" while "only her lips moved," which caused Eli, the priest, as he watched her with grave concern, to come to the conclusion that she was drunk. He questioned her regarding the matter, and she answered, "My Lord, I am a woman of a sorrowful spirit: I have drunk neither wine nor strong drink, but have poured out my soul before the Lord."

And today, centuries later, we read of Hannah, and we know how splendidly her prayer was answered and how faithfully she kept her promise to the Lord.

She brought her weaned child to the temple and left him there, saying to Eli, "Oh my lord, as thy soul liveth, I am the woman that stood by thee here, praying unto the Lord. For this child I prayed; and the Lord hath given me my petition which I asked of him. Therefore also I have lent him to the Lord; as long as he liveth he shall be lent to the Lord." And no doubt she added, "Take him now into the temple and rear him as thy own and bring him up in the nurture and admonition of the Lord."

Her song of praise is second only to one in its magnificence of beauty and phrasing. Mary's Magnificat and Hannah's hymn of praise may well stand out as the greatest compositions of women of all time.

Every mother knows that Hannah's sacrifice was not an easy one; to give up an only child, a mere baby, into the care of others would bring a wrench to the stoutest heart. Hannah's love for her son must have been greatly intensified by her long wait for his coming and her passionate need of a child. To keep her vow to lend him to the Lord meant giving him up entirely to the care of comparative strangers. It must have been truly a heartbreaking experience.

Yet Hannah paid her vow to the Lord with no word of complaint. We have no record of any regret she may have expressed because of her great sacrifice. Indeed there is an evident undercurrent of gladness through her days that blesses the heart of the reader.

There is no more tender and moving statement in all the Bible than this: "Moreover his mother made him a little coat, and brought it to him from year to year, when she came up with her husband to offer the yearly sacrifice." No mother can read these words without a contraction of the heart.

Think of it—the one little garment through the long year of separation! One can visualize her shaping the little coat, each stitch a mark of her great love. There must have been much tenderness in the handling of the soft material, much wistfulness as the completed garment was folded and laid away awaiting her yearly pilgrimage to the temple.

There is no woman whose heart would not be stirred with pity for that mother, and yet she was joyfully keeping her pact with God. The Lord must have been exceedingly pleased with Hannah.

To give a child to the Lord is no light matter. It is an earnest business which allows for no retraction. Oh, that more mothers today might so dedicate their children! Oh, that they might be faithful in keeping their part of the bargain by preparing themselves to be worthy leaders of the young! If this should be, the whole world would soon feel the blessed effects. The new generation would be God-minded and earnest followers of the right, and the earth would know a peace and harmony hitherto undreamed of.

We have in Hannah the highest type of motherhood. She prayed that she might have a child. She was willing and glad to lend him to the Lord. She did what she could to help by meeting his physical needs. This done, she left him with God.

As mothers we should realize the importance of giving our children early to him. Also—and this is most important—we should give God to our children. There is no greater gift that a mother could give a child than this, and it is never too early to give it.

Give the child a faith in the old, sweet, true, and beautiful story of the Christ Child's birth; teach him to love and trust that Child grown to manhood with his great love for all little children; give him the eternal hope of salvation which Christ offers; and having done all this, leave him to the watchful care of a God who is able to keep to the uttermost all that is entrusted to his care.

Our Father, may mothers everywhere learn much from Hannah of old. May their dedication of their children be as sincere as was hers. Help us to realize the vast importance of training a child in the way he should go, remembering that he will not depart from that way if the training be wise and right. God, we pray thee, bless all mothers everywhere. Give them the wisdom to please thee in the great work of rearing their children aright. Amen.

25

Meditation on the Twenty - Third Psalm

The Lord is my shepherd;

The pastures of the earth are green
   And beautiful, yet they grow dim
As night falls, and my timid heart
   Would fear if it were not for him
Who guides me with strong, gentle hands
Safely across life's meadowlands.

I shall not want.

I have not wanted hitherto;
   I shall not want while there is spread
Bright tablelands from which to dine
   And emerald grasses for my bed,
With stars above to satisfy
My beauty-loving spirit's cry.

He maketh me to lie down in green pastures:

My Shepherd knows when I am tired.
   He knows my every earthly need.

117

The late sun sinks beyond the hills,
   And I have need of rest indeed.
I lie me down contentedly;
He ever will watch over me.

He leadeth me beside the still waters.

The dawn is beautiful! I rise
   Refreshed from the long rest of night.
Thirsty for water now I turn,
   And there before me, clear and bright,
Lie clean, cool waters at whose brink
I fall upon my knees to drink.

He restoreth my soul:

A foolish one too often, I
   Spend strength that strips me of my power.
I rove too far, grow overtired,
   Lose faith and hope in some dark hour;
Then forced to rest awhile, I can
Rise strengthened for my tasks again.

He leadeth me in the paths of righteousness.

"For his name's sake" he bids me move
   Along the paths of right; he goes
Ever before me, pointing out
   The narrow pathway, for he knows
How prone I am to wander far
Where the rocks and tangled brambles are.

Yea, though I walk through the valley of the shadow of death,

"I will fear no evil," Shepherd mine,
  "For thou art with me" and will be
My keeper, my unfailing guide,
  Through time and all eternity.
Stay close beside me; thus I know
Quite brave and fearless I can go.

Thy rod and thy staff they comfort me.

Thy rod, thy staff, how straight and strong!
  And held within thy firm kind hand.
It comforts me, dear Lord, to know
  That as I journey down the land,
Though it be smooth or rutted sod,
I am guided by thy staff, thy rod.

Thou preparest a table before me.

"In the presence of mine enemies"
  He spreads a table that they may
Behold his mercies and return
  From fields that beckoned them astray,
That they too graciously may dine
Upon the good foods that are mine.

Thou anointest my head with oil;

My cup runs over with the clear,
  Good oil of mercy he bestows;

I kneel to worship at his feet—
How great the debt my glad heart owes!
Lord, I would serve thee all my days
Through grateful deeds, through prayer and
praise.

Surely goodness and mercy shall follow me
all the days of my life:

They shall follow me while I shall live;
Thy goodness and thy mercy, Lord.
Unmerited thy favor is
And undeserved thy rich reward;
But humbly now I kneel in prayer
To thank thee for thy constant care.

And I will dwell in the house of the Lord
for ever.

Forever! Vast eternal word!
The pastures of the earth are green,
But the heavenly lands are greener far
Than any earthly eye hath seen,
And though the eternal fields be wide,
Lord, thou wilt still be by my side.

Meditation on the Lord's Prayer

Our Father

We stand with bowed heads before the privilege that is ours of calling thee Father. We say the word over and over, savoring the depth of its meaning—"our *Father.*" It is a beautiful word, tender and strong and true, and summed up it spells the love of one for the helpless and the needy, and in thy case, dear Lord, it is a divine love.

Truly, our Father, we are utterly dependent upon thy care and thy tenderness. Without thee we would be as helpless as any little child deprived of the wisdom and the insight of his earthly parents.

Thou art both father and mother to us. There is no deviation in thy love. We rely upon thee for our needs. Our hands reach out to thee and find thy hand clasped about our own, and thus we can go forward safely and unafraid, assured that all will be well.

We thank thee and praise thee that thou hast

permitted us to call thee by the intimate and sacred name "Father."

Which art in heaven,

Lord, it is blessed to realize thy universality. Thy perpetual dwelling, we know, is in heaven, and yet we are certain that thou art with us here on earth, closer than our hands and feet and nearer than our breathing.

We can reach out and touch thy garment's hem with our hands. Thou art beside us on the street and at the fireside. Thou art ever close to all beds of pain.

Heaven is filled with thy radiance, and to all who have eyes to see that same radiance illuminates our days with its white perpetual light.

"Lo, I am with you alway," Christ said, and we know that thou wilt be with us through time and through the far reaches of eternity.

We praise thee, Lord, that thou hast considered thy earthly children's need and that we can share here on earth the glory of heaven. Help us ever to be worthy of thy hourly presence, and prepare us, we pray, for the blinding glory of eternity.

Hallowed be thy name.

Our Father, we would hold thy name apart as sacred. May it ever be hallowed. We know of thy kingly titles—Jehovah, Emmanuel, Lord, and God—yet we have thee for our Father! We are ever mindful that we are children of a king.

We would keep thy name holy. We utter it in our prayers. We call it aloud in times of great stress. We sing it in our praise, and we shout it in victories.

Never would we take thy blessed name in vain. We would cherish it in our hearts, and we would tell it abroad that others may come to know the joy and the intimacy of thy companionship. We would praise thy holy name at all times, for it is worthy to be praised.

Thy kingdom come.

Lord God, we pray most earnestly and sincerely that thy blessed kingdom may come in all its power and glory to this our hurt and troubled earth.

May it come into our individual hearts. Purify them with the clean winds from heaven, that they may be fit places for thee to dwell. We would be upright and righteous citizens of this earth and of that wondrous future kingdom. We would be fired with a quenchless zeal for the saving of souls! We would reach out and touch lives that know thee not and thus be instrumental in helping bring about that great transformation.

Open our eyes that we may see that we are largely responsible for the coming of thy kingdom. May we realize our responsibility and go foreward with thee to the accomplishment of this magnificent task. Lord God, soon may thy kingdom come on earth.

Thy will be done.

Our gracious heavenly Father, we would not falter here in our praying. We would say unhesitatingly, "Thy will be done in earth, as it is in heaven." Why should we shrink from the working of thy will? Why should we desire aught but that which is always right and best for us?

Thy will, Lord, has made heaven a perfect dwelling place. May it be carried out unfailingly on earth with no opposition from any of thy nearsighted and rebellious children.

Thou art farseeing. Thy eyes behold the end of the journey while ours but see the way. We would go forward knowing that what is thy will for us is a safeguard to our daily living, and that we can trust thee absolutely and at all times. Truly may thy will be done, O blessed one.

Give us this day our daily bread.

Our Father, as thou didst give thy children manna in their wilderness, thus, Lord, supply our needs in our wilderness of today. We do not ask for tomorrow's loaf, tomorrow's garments, tomorrow's shelter. We believe that as our day so shall our needs be met by thee.

We would especially evaluate the miracle of bread—the miracle that ever is wrought in one small loaf. Thou hast provided the soil, the seed, the sun, the rain, and the fuel for the oven's glowing fire. All are thy blessed provisions for us thy children.

We would ever be frugal, knowing that in thy great economy there is no room for waste. We would be generous in our sharing, remembering how often Christ thy Son, broke bread with the humble. We would offer up to thee our most grateful thanks for thy great and consistent gift of bread. We thank thee, gracious Lord, for this life-giving substance.

And forgive us our debts, as we forgive our debtors.

Lord God, so cleanse our hearts from malice and resentment against any living soul that we may safely pray this prayer.

We come to these thy words, and we should search deeply within our inmost hearts before we can be certain that we dare utter them. Is there bitterness there against any fellow man?

Is there hatred of another? Have we failed to forgive when we feel we may have been wronged? If so, our Father, help us to see that we dare not ask of thee what we have failed to do ourselves.

Grant, Lord, that we may be enabled to ask without hesitancy for thy forgiveness; for only as we forgive shall we be forgiven, and only thus can we know peace.

And lead us not into temptation,

Dear heavenly Father, thou knowest our innermost beings. Thou rememberest our feeble frames and that we are as the dust that is too often tossed about by every wind that blows.

Steady us, Lord, that we may pray for our deliverance from evil. Make a way for our escape from every threatening peril that may beset us. Give us the high courage to stand against temptation, and defend us in times of trouble.

Thus only, thou knowest, can we move forward without defeat. Only through thy strength can we be strong. Supply that strength, we pray thee.

But deliver us from evil:

Lord God, the evil influence of thy archenemy is abroad in the land. We know that he hates and fears all that is right and holy. He would hurt any child of thine if through that child he could hurt thy loving heart.

With thy powerful shielding arm push back the evil which threatens us and deliver us from that satanic might. Help us to stay our minds upon thee and upon all things that are lovely and pure and good, that nothing can come between us and thee. May we shun every harmful and hurtful thing—each pitfall, each danger to our immortal souls. Deliver us from evil, blessed Lord, throughout our entire lifetime, that we may come before thee worthy of thy loving care.

For thine is the kingdom, and the power, and the glory,

Like a great triumphant hymn lifting up to thee these words ring out, giving thee all praise, all power, all glory.

We kneel before the magnificence of their meaning. We are blinded by the celestial light as we contemplate the radiance enshrined within this brief phrasing. We adore thee. We love thee, and we would serve thee faithfully and humbly evermore.

Thy kingdom, thy power, thy glory are the lights ahead beckoning us onward and upward to the Celestial City. May we reach it, Lord, with undiminished strength as we journey.

For ever.

Forever with thee, blessed Lord! We stand'face skyward, striving to pierce the blue illimitable sky, to catch if possible a glimpse of the glory land; but our eyes are holden, and we cannot see.

We turn to survey the earthly roads that are yet to be traveled, and we pray most earnestly that we may draw nearer day by day to that bright haven ahead. Amen.